You shall have an evil son.
Your nation shall become prey
to terror and tears. Rivers of blood
will flow, the heads of the mighty
will fall. Your cities will be
devoured by flames.

Mark, Orthodox Patriarch of Jerusalem,
making a prophesy to the father of
Ivan the Terrible, 1526

This book is for my wife, Debra, and son, Zachary.

Photographs © 2008: akg-Images, London: 30, 67 top (Archiv f.Kunst & Geschichte), 68 center; Art Resource, NY: 67 center (Scala), 28, 66 top right, 109 (The New York Public Library); Bridgeman Art Library International Ltd., London/New York: 53, 63, 68 bottom (Central Naval Museum, St. Petersburg, Russia), 33 (Private Collection), 106 (Tretyakov Gallery, Moscow, Russia); Corbis Images: 71 top (Archivo Iconografico, SA), 10, 75, 105 (Bettmann), 69 top left, 81 (Johansen Krause/Archivo Iconografico, SA), 83 (Grigory Sedov/The State Russian Museum); Getty Images/Baron Mikhail Petrovich Klodt von Jurgensburg/The Bridgeman Art Library: 117; Mary Evans Picture Library: 17, 45, 60, 68 top, 94, 113, 118; North Wind Picture Archives: 66 bottom, 70 center; ShutterStock, Inc./ Svetlana Chernova: 69 top right; The Granger Collection, New York: 40, 51, 67 bottom (Rue de Archives), 22, 70 bottom, 71 bottom; The Image Works: 19, 37, 66 top left, 69 bottom, 70 bottom, 89 (Roger-Viollet), 87 (Topham).

Illustrations by XNR Productions, Inc.: 4, 5, 8, 9
Cover part, page 8 inset by Mark Summers
Chapter art by Raphael Montoliu

Library of Congress Cataloging-in-Publication Data

Price, Sean.
Ivan the Terrible : tsar of death / Sean Price.
p. cm. — (A wicked history)
Includes bibliographical references and index.
ISBN 13: 978-0-531-12597-7 (lib. bdg.) 978-0-531-20500-6 (pbk.)
ISBN 10: 0-531-12597-1 (lib. bdg.) 0-531-20500-2 (pbk.)
1. Ivan IV, Czar of Russia, 1530-1584—Juvenile literature. 2. Russia—Kings and rulers—Biography—Juvenile literature. 3. Russia—History—Ivan IV, 1533-1584—Juvenile literature. I. Title.
DK106.P75 2007
947'.043092—dc22
[B]

2007037474

Tod Olson, Series Editor
Marie O'Neill, Art Director
Allicette Torres, Cover Design
SimonSays Design!, Book Design and Production

© 2008 Scholastic Inc.

1 2 3 4 5 6 7 8 9 10 R 17 16 15 14 13 12 11 10 09 08   23

A WICKED HISTORY™

Ivan the Terrible

Tsar of Death

SEAN PRICE

Franklin Watts
An Imprint of Scholastic Inc.
New York   Toronto   London   Auckland   Sydney
Mexico City   New Delhi   Hong Kong
Danbury, Connecticut

The World of Tsar Ivan IV

As the first tsar of Russia, Ivan the Terrible
turned a new nation into an empire.

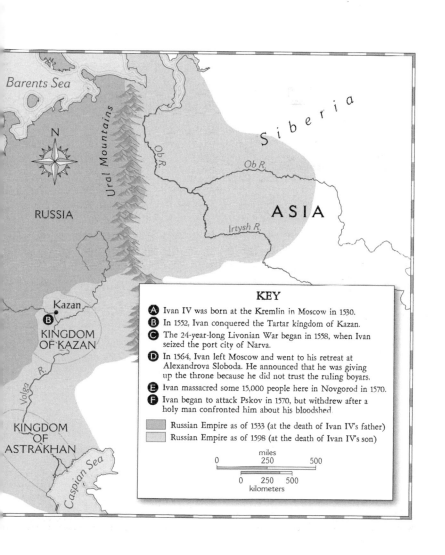

Barents Sea

N

Siberia

Ural Mountains

Ob R.

Ob R.

RUSSIA

ASIA

Irtysh R.

Kazan

KINGDOM
OF KAZAN

Volga R.

KINGDOM
OF
ASTRAKHAN

Caspian Sea

KEY

A Ivan IV was born at the Kremlin in Moscow in 1530.

B In 1552, Ivan conquered the Tartar kingdom of Kazan.

C The 24-year-long Livonian War began in 1558, when Ivan seized the port city of Narva.

D In 1564, Ivan left Moscow and went to his retreat at Alexandrova Sloboda. He announced that he was giving up the throne because he did not trust the ruling boyars.

E Ivan massacred some 15,000 people here in Novgorod in 1570.

F Ivan began to attack Pskov in 1570, but withdrew after a holy man confronted him about his bloodshed.

    Russian Empire as of 1533 (at the death of Ivan IV's father)

    Russian Empire as of 1598 (at the death of Ivan IV's son)

miles
0   250   500

0   250 500
kilometers

TABLE OF CONTENTS

The World of Tsar Ivan IV 4

A Wicked Web 8

Introduction 10

PART 1: A CHILDHOOD OF TERROR

CHAPTER 1: Orphaned 16

CHAPTER 2: Puppet Prince 23

CHAPTER 3: A Terrible Teenager 29

PART 2: YEARS OF SUCCESS

CHAPTER 4: The First Tsar 36

CHAPTER 5: A Fire for Reform 42

CHAPTER 6: A Fresh Start 46

CHAPTER 7: Conquering Kazan 49

CHAPTER 8: Feverish 55

CHAPTER 9: Sorrow Strikes 59

IVAN IV IN PICTURES 66

PART 3: TERROR UNLEASHED

CHAPTER 10: Mistrust and Murder 74

CHAPTER 11: The Pretend Abdication 78

CHAPTER 12: The Land Apart 84

CHAPTER 13: The Savior of Pskov 91

CHAPTER 14: End of the Oprichnina 97

PART 4: DECLINE AND FALL

CHAPTER 15: Disaster Strikes 104

CHAPTER 16: A Death in the Family 110

CHAPTER 17: Final Prayers 115

Wicked? 120

Timeline of Terror 122

Glossary 123

Find Out More 125

Index 126

Author's Note and Bibliography 128

A Wicked Web

A look at the allies and enemies of Tsar Ivan IV.

Ivan's Family and Friends

VASILY III
Ivan's father and
Grand Prince of
Russia

ELENA
Ivan's mother and
Grand Princess of
Russia

YURI
Ivan's younger brother

YURI GLINKSY
Ivan's uncle, and at
one time the leader
of a family that ran
Russia

ANASTASIA
Ivan's first and most
beloved wife

IVAN IV

DMITRI
Ivan's first son, who
died young

IVAN
Ivan's second son,
whom he killed

FEODOR
Ivan's third son, who
succeeded Ivan as tsar

MAKARY
head of the Russian
Orthodox Church

Ivan's Opponents and Critics

SHUISKY FAMILY
important family of boyars; led
by Andrei Shuisky

BELSKY FAMILY
another important boyar family;
competed with the Shuiskys for
control of Russia

FATHER SYLVESTER
led Ivan's early reforms—until
Ivan turned on him

ALEXEY ADASHEV
another adviser who fell out of
favor with Ivan

YEDIGER MAKHMET
Khan, or leader, of the
Kingdom of Kazan

DEVLET GUIREY
Khan of the Kingdom of Crimea;
in 1571 his army set fire to
Moscow

STEPHEN BATHORY
King of Poland and Lithuania

TSAR IVAN IV, 1530–1584

Novgorod, Russia, January 9, 1570

RUSSIA'S DEEP SNOW could not muffle the screams. Men and women prayed and pleaded for mercy. Boys and girls cried out in pain. Babies wailed in the cold winter air. The city of Novgorod was under assault. Its people were being massacred.

And the mastermind of the attack was their own king, Tsar Ivan IV.

Ivan had always been suspicious of the people of Novgorod. Unlike other Russians, they welcomed foreigners. They had once elected their own leaders. All of this was distasteful to Ivan. He did not trust foreigners. And he certainly did not believe in democracy. In his view, true leaders were chosen by God, not by the people.

Near the end of 1569, Ivan got word that Novgorod's leaders planned to hand their city over to Russia's archenemy, Poland, and ask to be ruled by the Polish king. The information was false. But it gave Ivan the excuse he needed to punish the people of Novgorod.

For six weeks that winter, Ivan's men looted Novgorod and tortured its residents. City and church leaders were accused of plotting against Ivan. They were tried, convicted, and executed, usually in a matter of days. Some were burned alive.

Others were taken to the frozen Volkhov River and thrown into holes in the ice. Ivan jeeringly asked one victim what he saw under the icy water. The gasping man replied that he saw the demons of Hell. Then he added that the demons would soon come for Ivan. The tsar had the man hauled out and boiled alive.

By the middle of February, Ivan's soldiers had stripped the city of food, clothing, and anything else they could carry. They even stole a set of beautiful carved wooden doors from Novgorod's cathedral. By the time they left, the army may have killed 15,000 people. Thousands more died of disease and hunger in the following year.

The massacre at Novgorod was Ivan's greatest single crime. But it was just one on a long list. Ivan killed easily. He imagined enemies around every corner. And he destroyed them ruthlessly. Other leaders from Ivan's time were no strangers to torture and execution. Yet even they saw Ivan as a monster.

For all his crimes, Ivan was admired for his accomplishments. He helped build Russia's empire. He attacked wealthy nobles who exploited ordinary Russians. Even before Novgorod, Russians had begun calling their tsar Ivan Grozny. This translates into English as "Ivan the Terrible." In the 15th century, terrible meant fearsome or awesome. Ivan's nickname was a sign of fear—but also respect.

How did Russia's first tsar become one of the most feared and powerful leaders in history? The answers begin in 1530, the year of Ivan's birth. . . .

PART 1

A Childhood of Terror

CHAPTER 1

Orphaned

Ivan learns to survive ON HIS OWN.

SUDDEN, VIOLENT THUNDERSTORMS raged across Russia the day Ivan the Terrible came into the world. He was born around 6:00 P.M. on August 25, 1530. Bells rang out in the city of Moscow to welcome the new crown prince. Russians flocked to churches to give thanks.

Ivan's birth was a triumph for his father, Grand Prince Vasily III. The 51-year-old prince ruled over an ever-expanding nation founded by his father, Ivan III. Vasily had waited years for a son who could extend the family's reign. Now, thanks to his second wife, Elena Glinskaya, he had one. Two years later, he had another son, a boy named Yuri.

But the new father's joy was short-lived. In 1533, he noticed a small sore on his leg. It turned into a pus-filled boil. The boil grew and stank horribly. Vasily's doctors used a common cure of the time. They bled the grand prince and poured vodka on the boil. They

FOR MANY YEARS Vasily III, the Grand Prince of Moscow, had no heir. His second wife, Elena Glinskaya, gave birth to Ivan in 1530. '

succeeded only in weakening their patient, and before long, Vasily had a terrible case of blood poisoning.

The grand prince prepared to die. He prayed and kissed portraits of saints. He also made arrangements for his eldest son to succeed him as grand prince.

At age three, Ivan was obviously not ready to rule. So Vasily appointed a council of advisers to run the country and look after Ivan. The seven men on the council were all *boyars*—noblemen who ran the government and military. Ivan would need their help until he reached the age of 15. Then he would take control of all the lands ruled by the grand prince.

When Ivan's father died in December 1533, the council officially took over. But Ivan's mother Elena was the real force behind the throne. She kept a ruthless hold on power. "No one came out of the dungeons alive," one observer wrote. Elena even threw her own uncle, Mikhail Glinsky, into prison for meddling in her affairs.

But Elena's reign did not last long. She died suddenly on April 3, 1538. Many people suspected poison. Ivan himself later blamed witchcraft.

Elena's death launched a violent power struggle. Two boyar families—the Shuiskys and the Belskys— fought for control of the throne. The goal for both sides was simple: Turn Ivan into a puppet prince. He

IVAN BECAME GRAND PRINCE when he was three years old, but his mother, Elena, was the real power behind the throne. Here, Ivan and Elena (seated at the top left) oversee the making of new coins.

would perform the role of ruler in public. But the boyars would make the decisions in private.

In their attempt to control the young prince, the boyars turned Ivan's childhood into a nightmare. When Elena died, Ivan became an orphan. His only source of support was his nanny, Agrafena. Ivan loved Agrafena dearly. But the boyars feared that she would get in the way of their plans. Within days of Elena's death, armed men came to take Agrafena away. Seven-year-old Ivan held onto his nanny's skirt. He sobbed and screamed. He begged the guards to leave her. They simply shoved him aside.

Agrafena was sent to a convent. Ivan never saw her again.

The grand prince now had no protectors. His brother Yuri, who was deaf and mute, became his only playmate.

At public ceremonies, Russia's boyars treated Ivan like royalty. They referred to themselves as his slaves and asked his permission to speak. But in private, they abused the boy. They stole his parents' belongings. They handled Ivan and Yuri roughly. Sometimes they simply neglected the boys.

Ivan later recalled how the boyars "kept us in dire poverty." They made him wear old clothes, handed down from their own sons. One day, Prince Ivan Shuisky took over Vasily's bedroom. He gave Ivan a lecture while sitting on the bed with his foot on the pillow. "He . . . adopted toward me, the tsar and sovereign, a contemptuous attitude," Ivan wrote.

The young prince would remember these insults for the rest of his life.

THE BOYARS AND THE GRAND PRINCE

IN IVAN'S TIME, Moscow's grand prince shared power with about 150 noble families around the country. Members of these families were called boyars. They held the highest government and military jobs in Russia. They also owned most of the land. Many of the country's eight or nine million people paid rent to live and grow crops on boyar estates.

For hundreds of years, the boyars had ruled their own lands without interference from Moscow. Ivan's grandfather, also a grand prince, had brought them all under his control. He and Ivan's father consulted the boyars on important decisions. But in Ivan's view, the grand prince alone was meant to rule Russia.

BOYARS IN FRONT OF THE KREMLIN

CHAPTER 2

Puppet Prince

A scared boy survives
A NASTY CHILDHOOD.

ONE MORNING IN JANUARY 1542, Ivan was awakened suddenly at 6:00 A.M. A priest named Josef barged into his room. The priest was terrified and begged Ivan to protect him.

Josef was the *metropolitan*, or leader, of the official church of Russia, the Russian Orthodox Church. Normally, the metropolitan was the second-most powerful man in Russia, after the grand prince himself.

But with the boyars battling for power, these were not normal times. Josef had supported the

Belskys in their struggle against the Shuiskys. Now, he was about to pay for his decision.

Minutes after Josef burst into Ivan's bedroom, a group of the Shuiskys' followers came after him. According to one account, the men beat Josef before Ivan's eyes. They dragged him away screaming.

Ivan could do nothing. The 11-year-old prince was left huddled in his bed, wondering whether he would be next.

Ivan survived for years like this. Neither the Shuiskys nor the Belskys could get a firm hold on power. Ivan was useful to both families because the common people accepted him as their ruler. As a result, he escaped assassination.

Meanwhile, the government in Moscow plunged into chaos. No one was able to take charge.

Before long, lawlessness spread throughout Russia. Public officials took bribes. They raised taxes to increase their personal wealth. Armed gangs roamed Moscow and the countryside. Farmers and merchants found it hard to do business safely. People began to go hungry, and they blamed the boyars for their misery. "There is no order in the land," one Italian visitor said. "The state barely exists."

Ivan knew little about the country's problems. He lived hidden from it all in a huge compound called the Kremlin. He had almost no power over important decisions. But as grand prince, he had to appear for formal events. He dressed in long, heavy robes to sit through religious ceremonies or meet foreign ambassadors. "I was never free to do anything," he later wrote. "I could never do what I wanted or what a boy should."

In private, Ivan's council watched him carefully. They knew he would soon be old enough to rule. They wanted control over his friends and advisers. As a result, Ivan had few playmates. He was surrounded by adult guards and servants. Most of them served as spies for the Shuiskys or the Belskys.

In 1542, Prince Andrei Shuisky emerged as the most powerful boyar. Shuisky watched suspiciously as Ivan developed a friendship with a man named Feodor Vorontzov. Finally, the boyar couldn't stand it any longer. Shuisky and his men got into an argument with Vorontzov. They beat Ivan's friend and sent him off to prison.

For Ivan, it was a moment of decision. He was 13 years old. He felt sure that he was the rightful ruler of Russia. And yet the Shuiskys and the other boyars did as they pleased.

Ivan had finally had enough. Around Christmastime that year, according to one story, the boyars gathered at the Kremlin for a feast. Ivan decided to take a chance. He stood up and addressed the boyars. He accused them of destroying the country. They stole from the people, he claimed. They put prisoners to death without proof of their crimes. One man among them, he said, was the worst criminal of all: Andrei Shuisky.

Ivan ordered Shuisky arrested. None of the boyars moved to stop him. Guards seized Prince Shuisky, who was beaten to death and fed to the hounds. Shuisky's remains were left outside for two hours for others to see. Thirty boyars close to Shuisky were hanged as well. "From this moment the boyars began to fear and obey the sovereign," Russia's official history noted.

THE KREMLIN

IVAN GREW UP IN A GIANT CASTLE built to protect Moscow from invasion. The castle, or Kremlin, was a triangular fortress that stood in the center of the city. It overlooked the Moscow River from the top of a small hill.

By Ivan's time, the Kremlin was the home of Russia's leaders. It had developed into a 65-acre compound of buildings that included cathedrals, government offices, and palaces. The Kremlin was a town in itself. It had its own shops and even its own graveyards. Cannons jutted out from the high walls to protect the royal family against invaders and angry subjects.

THE WALLS OF THE KREMLIN
surrounded a bustling town.

CHAPTER 3

A Terrible Teenager

The terrified prince becomes
A SAVAGE ADOLESCENT.

THE BRUTAL KILLING OF ANDREI SHUISKY made it clear: Ivan was no longer a boy, helpless and terrified. By 13, he was six feet tall with a broad chest and long, thin arms. He loved to hunt. Few joys matched galloping full-speed across the Russian countryside. Giant hunting parties followed the young prince on horseback while he tracked bears, wolves, and foxes.

Ivan loved the chase. And he also loved the kill. He got a sick pleasure from the pain of other creatures. He

AT 16, IVAN WAS OLD ENOUGH to run the country but showed little interest. One of his favorite pastimes was to lead a gang of friends through Kremlin Square, trampling the peasants of Moscow.

sometimes threw cats and dogs off the Kremlin walls to watch them suffer.

In 1546, both the Shuiskys and the Belskys lost their grip on power. Ivan's mother's family, the Glinskys, took over. The Glinskys and Ivan struck a deal. They would run the country while he ran wild.

The grand prince formed a gang made up of teenage nobles. Together, they roamed Moscow's streets, causing trouble.

Kremlin Square, just outside the palace walls, was Moscow's main marketplace. There, traders bargained over melons, fox furs, leather boots, knives, and other goods. Ivan and his companions rode whooping through this mass of people. Those who got in their way were trampled and whipped.

Despite his violent streak, Ivan considered himself to be very religious. Like many Russians, he went to church often. He prayed before the candle-lit images of saints, called icons. He bowed in the flickering light, his arms spread wide, his face to the stone floor.

Ivan also became a passionate student. At the time, few Russians—maybe one in a thousand—could read and write. Those who learned did so by memorizing and repeating religious songs and prayers. Ivan probably learned this way, too. He also studied the lives of the saints and could recite long passages from the Bible.

Not all of Ivan's education came from books or teachers. The deadly power struggles he grew up with made a deep impression. "I adopted the devious ways of the people around me," Ivan later wrote. "I learned to be crafty like them."

The people around Ivan saw a bright, handsome young man. He showed talent as a musician, a writer, and a public speaker. But he was also dangerously unstable. One day, he might laugh and act like everybody's friend. Another day he might feel holy and quiet. The next day, he might order a boyar's tongue cut out for speaking rudely.

At 16, this unpredictable boy was about to take control of Russia.

A Nation Under God

IN IVAN'S TIME, RUSSIANS WERE A DEEPLY RELIGIOUS PEOPLE. Almost everyone wore a cross and carried prayer beads. Homes and shops displayed icons. Visitors generally looked for the holy images when they entered a new place. When they saw an icon, they crossed themselves three times. Then they bowed and muttered, "O Lord, have mercy."

Rituals were very important in the Russian Orthodox Church. Religious services often lasted for four hours. The faithful ate meat only three times a week. Russian women hid their skin under red and white paint to avoid tempting men into sin. And all Russian men wore beards in imitation of Jesus. Anyone who shaved was denied a religious burial.

AN ICON OF MARY AND THE BABY JESUS

PART 2

Years of Success

CHAPTER 4

The First Tsar

IVAN TAKES OVER, gets a new title, and marries his first wife.

GOLD SPARKLED in the thin winter light. Ivan himself seemed to glow from the gold cloth and precious gems he wore. The boyars and the clergy, too, were in fine dress for the occasion.

On January 16, 1547, this proud group crowded into Moscow's Cathedral of the Assumption. Most of the Glinskys were there. They still held many of the ruling positions in the country. But Ivan had finally come of age. He was about to be crowned as the true leader of Russia.

IN 1547 IVAN WAS PROCLAIMED "Tsar and Monarch of all the Russias." The event was modeled after ceremonies from the ancient Roman Empire.

As the coronation began, bells rang. Choirs sang. Russians crossed themselves and bowed as Ivan strode by on a velvet carpet. Metropolitan Makary, the new head of the Orthodox Church, led the ceremony.

Makary placed the fur-lined crown on Ivan's head. Ivan also received a royal scepter, a cape, and a few splinters of wood that were said to have come from the cross on which Jesus was killed

"Long years to noble Ivan, the good, the honorable, the favorite of God," Makary recited. "Grand Prince of Vladimir and Moscow, Tsar and Monarch of all the Russias."

One of those titles—*tsar*—was new. The word comes from the Roman title *caesar*, or emperor. Ivan took it in part to announce that he wanted greater authority over the boyars. But Ivan was also declaring that, like the great Roman emperors, he planned to create a great empire.

Such a powerful man must have an heir. So Ivan began to look for a wife. By tradition, the search was done by holding a bride show. The Glinskys sent agents to inspect possible brides all over Russia. The most promising were sent to Moscow for the show.

The nervous girls arrived at the Kremlin. When the time came, they stood before Ivan dressed in their finest robes. Some were as young as 12, the legal age for marriage in Russia. Many painted their fingernails and wore red and white makeup. Each girl curtsied deeply before the tsar on his throne.

When he had seen all the girls, Ivan chose a winner. He presented her with a handkerchief embroidered with gold, silver, and pearls. The girl's name was Anastasia Romanovna Zakharina. Russia's first tsarina came from a royal family. She was beautiful and kind. Ivan genuinely seemed to love her and nicknamed her his "little heifer."

Others liked Anastasia as well. She settled in quickly at the Kremlin. Some people felt she had a calming effect on Ivan. An English explorer later noticed it when he visited Moscow. Ivan, he said, was

ANASTASIA EMBRACES HER HUSBAND. The tsarina was said
to help keep Ivan calm, but he still showed signs of terrible cruelty.

"young and riotous." But Anastasia "ruled him with [gentleness] and wisdom."

The Englishman, however, may have overstated Anastasia's influence. In June 1547, soon after the wedding, a group of men from the city of Pskov arrived at Ivan's country home. Like many Russians, they were unhappy with the way the country was run. The local governor in Pskov was corrupt, they complained. They insisted that something be done.

According to one story, Ivan was outraged that the men would dare to complain to him. He had them seized. He ordered his guards to pour alcohol on their heads and light their beards on fire. It seemed certain that the men would be killed.

Suddenly a messenger rode into view. The giant bell in the Kremlin had fallen, he said. Nobody knew why.

The news must be an omen, Ivan decided, a sign of terrible things to come. He left at once to investigate. The men from Pskov were released.

CHAPTER 5

A Fire for Reform

Ivan moves to help his people—
AND INCREASE HIS POWER.

Not long after Ivan returned to Moscow, the city was rocked by a disaster. On June 21, Moscow's Church of the Holy Cross burst into flames.

The firestorm spread rapidly. A strong wind whipped up giant waves of fire. The flames carried over the Kremlin's walls and across the city. Ivan and his court fled across the Moscow River to safety. Behind them, the raging fire destroyed building after building, including Ivan's palace. Dramatic explosions shook the city as the flames reached the gunpowder in the state arsenal.

Moscow lay in ashes. The fire killed nearly 2,000 people. Thousands more were left homeless. A cloud of smoke hung over the city for days.

Under the smoke, years of anger at the boyar rulers of Russia turned to open rebellion. Rumors spread that the Glinskys were responsible for the fire. Some people even blamed witchcraft. The Glinskys had supposedly ripped hearts from human bodies and soaked them in water. Then they sprinkled the liquid around the city, and it burst into flames.

Just days after the fire, a crowd gathered in the Kremlin Square. They chased Yuri Glinsky, Ivan's uncle, through the burned-out streets. Glinsky ducked into a cathedral to hide. But the rioters had no mercy. They killed the boyar near the church altar.

Yuri Glinsky's death sparked a full-scale riot. The mob went after any Glinsky ally it could find. In three days, the trail led the rioters to Ivan's home outside Moscow. Outraged, Ivan ordered the leaders of the uprising killed on the spot. Soldiers charged, and the mob fled. But the people of Moscow had accomplished their goal. The Glinskys' hold over Russia was broken.

Ivan was shocked. First his capital had burned. Now he faced a near revolution. Almost overnight, the young tsar became a serious leader.

Ivan turned to one of the few people he trusted, the Metropolitan Makary. With Makary's help, Ivan gathered a small group of advisers. These men became known as the "Chosen Council." Two of the council members emerged as Ivan's closest allies.

The first was Father Sylvester. He was a Russian Orthodox priest from Novgorod. Sylvester spoke firmly to the tsar. Ivan's cruelty, he said, had offended God. He reminded Ivan of his violent rides through the streets of Moscow and of his brutality toward the men of Pskov and others. Russia was now being punished for Ivan's crimes, Sylvester claimed. It was harsh criticism, yet Ivan trusted Sylvester.

AFTER A FIRE AND AN UPRISING nearly destroyed Moscow, Ivan was deeply shaken. At Father Sylvester's urging, the tsar (shown here on his knees) re-committed himself to God.

Aleksei Adashev emerged as the Chosen Council's other leader. Adashev's kindness was widely admired. It was said that he helped care for lepers in his own home. He was like an angel, one admirer wrote.

These men set out to reform Ivan's kingdom and to protect it from enemies.

CHAPTER 6

A Fresh Start

The tsar's new laws
CREATE AN ERA OF CHANGE.

UNDER THE INFLUENCE of his new advisers, Ivan made his mark on Russia.

He began to plan a series of new laws to curb the power of the nobility and the church. In 1549, he called together an assembly of boyars and church leaders. He gathered them all in Kremlin Square before the people of Moscow. Then, the young tsar rose to speak. He accused the boyars of abusing their power. "How many tears have you caused to be shed?" he demanded. "How many times have you made blood flow?"

Then he turned to the people in the crowd. He asked their forgiveness and promised to protect them from harm. "Starting from this day," he announced, "I shall be your judge and your defender!"

The tsar ended his performance by asking the people for complaints. He had Adashev set up a special office to receive them all. Petitions poured into Moscow from all across the land. People complained about high taxes and crime. They named corrupt officials and priests. They told stories of desperate poverty.

Ivan's Chosen Council responded with a series of reforms. The changes gave some relief to the common people. Mostly, they took power from the boyars and the church—and gave it to the tsar.

First, the council demanded that the tsar's laws be enforced throughout Russia. Until Ivan's reign, many villages simply ignored decrees from Moscow.

The council also promised tougher punishments for criminals, including corrupt government officials.

The church was forced to appeal to the tsar before obtaining more land. And priests who could read and write were ordered to open schools for the people.

Many of Ivan's reforms were designed to bring all of Russia under the tsar's control. But Ivan also wanted to educate his people. At the time, western Europe was far more advanced than Russia. Explorers from Spain, Portugal, and England sailed the seas in search of new lands. Scholars studied at universities full of books from the newly invented printing press. Workshops produced modern cannons and other weapons that Russian craftsmen could only dream about.

The tsar himself had good reason to dream of such things. Ivan needed military technology to accomplish another great goal. He wanted to expand his empire. Russia was surrounded by hostile countries. To the west lay Poland, Sweden, and Lithuania. To the south and east lay Russia's most feared and hated enemies, the Tartar khanates (or kingdoms). To extend his power, Ivan was ready to go to war with the Tartars.

CHAPTER 7

Conquering Kazan

IVAN TAKES ON
Russia's oldest enemies.

EACH SPRING, TERROR CAME TO RUSSIA with the sudden sound of hoofbeats. Tartar horsemen swept down on villages and cities. These gifted horsemen seemed to spring out of the ground on their short, strong ponies. They filled the air with arrows, making it dangerous to flee. Yet Russians who stayed behind were often murdered in their homes.

The Tartars burned villages, drove off cattle, and carried away crops. They also snatched children and sold them into slavery. Blonde-haired, blue-

SOLDIERS OF THE *STRELTSY* WERE ARMED with an
early kind of rifle. Ivan created this elite force by recruiting
volunteers from the peasant population.

eyed Russians fetched high prices in the slave markets of Asia and the Mediterranean.

Then, as quickly as the horsemen came, they disappeared.

Ivan and his advisers were determined to stop the Tartar raids. They raised taxes to support a bigger army. Then they created units of professional musketeers, called *streltsy*, or shooters. Ivan chose his officers based on their skill, not their rank among the nobility.

Ivan was building a war machine. His first and biggest target was the Tartar kingdom of Kazan.

The kingdom's capital, also called Kazan, was one of the most impressive cities in the world. With a population of 100,000, it was as big as London at the time. It sat high on a cliff over the Volga River. From across the river, its beautiful white and blue towers could be seen over its thick fortress walls.

Conquering Kazan would accomplish two things for Russia. A victory would stop some of the Tartar raids. It would also bring Christianity to Kazan. The Tartars there were Muslim, and most Russians felt it was their religious duty to convert as many as possible to Christianity.

Ivan had already attacked Kazan three times during his reign. He failed each time. By 1552, he was ready to strike again.

Ivan arrived outside of Kazan on August 23 with 100,000 soldiers. The city's fortress was defended by 30,000 troops. Another 35,000 Tartar troops patrolled the lands outside the city walls.

Ivan and his generals surrounded Kazan and tried to cut off its supplies. But a huge storm destroyed tons of food and gunpowder. The Russian camps became soggy, bug-infested bogs. Ivan's troops tried to charge the city. But archers on the walls showered them with arrows. Russian cannons blasted the fortress. But its walls would not budge.

The Russians refused to give in. They cut off Kazan's water supply. The troops and civilians inside

THE DEFEATED KHAN, Yediger Makhmet, kneels before
Ivan in October 1552, after the tsar and his army destroyed
the city of Kazan. Ivan spared the khan's life, but most of
the city's inhabitants were killed or sold into slavery.

Kazan suffered terribly but refused to give up. The Russians then dug two tunnels under the city's great wall. At dawn on October 2, they exploded gunpowder in the tunnels. Two gaping holes in the city walls opened up. Russians poured through.

Ivan almost missed his greatest victory. He dressed for the battle in his best armor. But he spent the day in prayer while the battle raged. Aides begged him to appear on the battlefield to inspire the troops. Finally, they got the frightened tsar onto a horse and led him to a spot where he was safe but could be seen from the battlefield.

Ivan's army won the battle by early afternoon. Soldiers moved through the city, killing men, women, and children. They captured Kazan's leader, Khan Yediger Makhmet. The khan, his wife, and his aides were brought to Ivan in chains. They fell to their knees before Ivan. The tsar was overjoyed by the sight. He agreed to spare their lives. The khan's chains were removed, and he rose to kiss Ivan's stirrup.

CHAPTER 8

Feverish

A SICKNESS TESTS THE LOYALTY
of Ivan's advisers.

IVAN'S VICTORY DID NOT END the Tartar threat to Russia. It would take five years to conquer the region around Kazan. And the Crimean Tartars to the south still threatened the Russians.

But the defeat of Kazan captured the imagination of Ivan's people. Songs and legends about Ivan's victory sprang up even before he returned to Moscow. The tsar's return journey was one long victory parade. Peasants lined the roads and riverbanks, cheering and bowing before the tsar.

Along the way, a messenger brought joyous news from Moscow. Ivan's wife, Anastasia, had given birth to a son, Dmitri. Ivan already had a daughter named Maria. But as a girl, Maria could not inherit the throne when Ivan died. A son meant that the tsar had an heir. Ivan was overjoyed. He gave the messenger his own cloak and horse for bringing such good news.

Huge crowds awaited Ivan in Moscow. "Long live our God-fearing tsar, conqueror of barbarians, savior of Christians!" they shouted. Ivan bowed from horseback as people pressed forward to kiss his hands and feet.

The feast celebrating the victory lasted three days. Ivan gave gifts to those who had fought in the battle. Favorites received furs, horses, and even land. "No man had ever seen such . . . generosity in the Kremlin palace," wrote the palace historian.

Yet in the months after Kazan, people noticed a change in the tsar. He was a war hero now, and he seemed drunk with arrogance. He was convinced that the boyars were plotting against him as they had when he was a child. He began to threaten them openly with revenge. He told one group of noblemen that after conquering Kazan he was powerful enough to do as he pleased. "Now," he said, "I am free to inflict upon you my torment and my wrath!"

The tsar had begun to imagine that he was surrounded by enemies. What happened next only confirmed his suspicions. In March 1553, Ivan was struck with a raging fever. For a time he felt certain he would die. Like his father, he worried about his son and heir. At one point he called his Chosen Council to his bedside. He demanded that the men kiss a cross and swear their loyalty to Dmitri.

The council members began to argue. Dmitri was just a baby. A council of boyars would have to rule for him. What would prevent Russia from returning to the violence and chaos of Ivan's youth? Many of the council members refused to support Dmitri. They wanted Ivan's adult cousin, Prince Vladimir Staritsky, to follow Ivan as tsar.

Ivan was stunned. Members of his own Chosen Council had refused to follow his orders. Adashev sided with Ivan. But Father Sylvester, his spiritual adviser, backed Staritsky.

Before a decision was reached, Ivan's health began to improve. Terrified of the tsar's vengeance, the boyars rushed to pledge their support to Dmitri.

Life in the Kremlin seemed to return to normal. The tsar did not take revenge against his council members. But he had not forgotten their betrayal.

By May, Ivan had fully regained his health. He decided to leave the difficult business of government behind for a time. He gathered his family and left for a monastery to give thanks to God for his recovery.

Tragedy struck on the return trip. Ivan's family was boarding a ship on the Sheksna River. The gangplank wobbled. Dmitri's nurse stumbled. She dropped the heir to the Russian throne into the river. Everyone tried frantically to save him. But they were too late. Nine-month-old Dmitri was dead.

CHAPTER 9

Sorrow Strikes

IVAN WINS VICTORIES ABROAD
but suffers the biggest loss of all
at home.

IN JUNE 1553, IVAN RETURNED to Moscow to bury his son. Dmitri was laid to rest at the feet of his grandfather, Vasily III. Ivan was devastated. The triumph at Kazan must have seemed like a distant memory.

But only nine months later, good news arrived again. Anastasia gave birth to another son. Once again, the tsar had an heir. This time he named the boy Ivan.

ENGLISH EXPLORER RICHARD CHANCELLOR is received
by Tsar Ivan. Their meeting led to a trade agreement between
Russia and England.

With his family crisis in the past for now, Ivan returned to the business of governing Russia. His conquest of Kazan had given him an empire. But he wanted more—much more. He wanted to open his backward country to the rest of the world.

The first new victory came easily. With Kazan in hand, the tsar went after its neighbor to the south. He sent an army down the Volga River into the Tartar kingdom of Astrakhan. The kingdom fell in July 1554. Its collapse gave Ivan control of the Volga, all the way to the Caspian Sea. As expected, trade with Asia boomed.

Western Europe, too, seemed to be opening its doors to Russia. In December 1553, an explorer from England named Richard Chancellor arrived in Moscow. The English and the Russians knew very little about each other. Some Englishmen believed fantastic stories about the Russians. According to one tale, a bizarre "vegetable lamb" grew in Russia. This odd creature was said to look like a small green sheep and grew on a stalk like a plant.

Chancellor was able to give the English more reliable information about Russia. His voyage also opened important trade routes between the two countries. And when Elizabeth I became queen of England, Ivan began a long correspondence with her.

But Ivan's merchants still had trouble getting through to the west. The Baltic Sea offered trading ships a clear route to Germany and the rest of Europe. But Russia's ports on the sea were clogged with ice in the winter.

Ivan knew what he wanted—access to the Baltic year-round. He also knew how to get it. On the Baltic, where Latvia and Estonia are today, lay the country of Livonia. Its rich ports were far enough south to stay free of ice. If the tsar could get his hands on them, Russian merchants would be able to sail freely to western Europe whenever they pleased.

Ivan wanted to go to war with Livonia. Sylvester and Adashev advised against it, but Ivan refused to listen.

THE RUSSIAN ARMY storms the city of Narva. Ivan's conquest
of this seaport allowed his merchants to trade directly with powers
in western Europe

In January 1558, 40,000 Russian troops marched
into Livonia. They seized the port city of Narva in
March. Almost immediately, goods from western
Europe poured into Russia. Russian merchants wept
with joy at the sight of so many trading ships.

But the Livonian War was far from over. The
Poles, the Swedes, and the Danes threatened to join
the battle. The fighting would drag on for the next

two decades. In 1559, when Ivan was forced into a truce, he lashed out in anger at his advisers.

Ivan could not control his temper in the best of times. Now the outbursts came more easily and more often. It didn't help that the Livonian crisis came at the same time as another personal tragedy. Anastasia was dying.

Anastasia had given Ivan six children, three girls and three boys. Only two had survived to see a second birthday. But they were both boys. Feodor, born in 1557, was just a toddler. Ivan was growing into a tall, handsome boy like his father.

Feodor's birth had weakened Anastasia. By 1559, it became clear that some disease was killing her. Both she and Ivan searched for a cure. Ivan brought in a woman from Livonia who supposedly had healing powers. Special icons were carried to the tsarina's bed. Ivan bargained with God. He prayed that he would give up Livonia if only his wife could be cured.

Nothing worked. The tsarina died on August 7, 1560. Thousands of mourners followed the carriage bearing her coffin. Ivan sobbed and wailed as he walked behind it. He beat his chest with his fists. Two men had to support him to keep him from collapsing.

Anastasia was buried in a nun's graveyard inside the Kremlin. With her went the best restraint on her husband's terrible rage.

Tsar Ivan IV in Pictures

PUPPET PRINCE
Still just a boy, Ivan (seated to the left) greets ambassadors from the Polish king. Ivan became grand prince when he was three.

ORPHAN IN THE KREMLIN
Ivan's mother died when he was seven, leaving him an orphan. He grew up here, in a huge compound called the Kremlin.

NATION OF NOBLES
Wealthy boyars, with their fine robes and expensive fur hats, owned most of Russia. When Ivan was a child, they battled for control of the country.

REBELLIOUS PRINCE

As a teenager, Ivan was a passionate student and a devout Christian. But he was also cruel and selfish. With his gang of young nobles, the prince terrorized the streets of Moscow.

RUSSIAN CAESAR

This fur-lined crown was already hundreds of years old when Ivan first wore it, at his coronation as tsar in 1547.

HAPPY COUPLE

Ivan the Terrible was devoted to Anastasia Romanovna, his beautiful first wife.

IVAN REPENTS

After a series of disasters almost destroyed Russia, a member of Ivan's Chosen Council spoke out against Ivan's cruelty. Here, the tsar goes on his knees to beg God's forgiveness.

WAR MACHINE

Ivan enlarged his army by recruiting peasants to serve as paid, professional soldiers. Soon, he could send 100,000 troops into battle.

IVAN THE CONQUEROR

For hundreds of years, the Tartars had taxed Russian towns and kidnapped peasants to sell as slaves. In 1552, Ivan struck back and destroyed Kazan, a Tartar city the size of London.

THE TERRIBLE

After his conquest of Kazan, Ivan became arrogant and paranoid. The deaths of his son and wife made things even worse.

SYMBOL OF POWER

To celebrate his victory over Kazan, Ivan commissioned St. Basil's Cathedral (above). According to legend, Ivan had his architect blinded to prevent the man from building anything to rival it.

PRETENDING TO QUIT

In 1564, Ivan retreated to his country home. He threatened to give up the throne unless given a guarantee of absolute power.

TERRIBLE MASSACRE

In 1570, Ivan suspected that Novgorod was planning to defect to Poland, so he set fire to the city. He also ordered the massacre of thousands of people.

ENSLAVING THE PEOPLE

Russian peasants had always been able to choose their own landlord. But Ivan turned them into serfs, a status little better than slavery.

STATE OF FEAR

Ivan leads supposed traitors to their execution, with the head of another victim impaled on his lance.

DEATH OF AN HEIR

Wracked with guilt, Ivan sits by his son's deathbed. The tsar cracked his heir's skull during a fit of rage.

THE TYRANT FALLS

Threatened with death if they were wrong, fortunetellers supposedly predicted the day of Ivan's death. The tsar saved them by collapsing on cue while playing chess.

PART 3

Terror Unleashed

CHAPTER 10

Mistrust and Murder

With Ivan's wife dead, THE TSAR'S CRUELTY BEGINS TO SURFACE.

IVAN TURNED 30 THE YEAR HIS WIFE DIED. After her death, Ivan began to see enemies everywhere. Father Sylvester and Adashev were the first to go. Over time, Ivan had grown to mistrust his two closest advisers. He suspected them both of plotting against him when he was sick in 1553. And he was furious with them for opposing the Livonian

IVAN WAS CONVINCED that his advisers Sylvester and
Adashev had poisoned his wife. He accused the men of
witchcraft and had them killed.

War. Now, he became convinced that Sylvester and Adashev had always hated his wife. Surely, he thought, they had helped to cause her death.

Within six weeks of Anastasia's funeral, Ivan put the two men on trial. The charges included witchcraft. Metropolitan Makary protested that neither man was allowed to speak in his own defense. But Ivan ignored the old scholar. He made sure that both men were found guilty.

Sylvester was exiled to an island in the White Sea, near the Arctic Circle. He died there mysteriously. Adashev was put in jail. He died two months later, either of disease or poison.

Many allies of Adashev and Sylvester were punished as well. Adashev's brother, Daniel, had served heroically in many of Ivan's military victories. But he and his 12-year-old son were arrested and executed. A Polish woman who knew Adashev was also murdered—along with her five sons.

About a year after Anastasia's death, Ivan took

another wife, a woman named Maria. But this marriage did not have the calming influence of the first. Ivan began hosting wild parties in the Kremlin. Clowns, dwarves, jesters, and acrobats entertained the tsar and his guests. At one masked ball, a boyar named Prince Mikhail Repnin refused to wear a mask. Ivan drunkenly tried to force one on him. Repnin threw it on the floor and stomped on it. "Is it fitting for a monarch to play the clown?" he said. Ivan threw him out of the room. Days later, the tsar had Repnin knifed to death in church.

Ivan knew that his behavior had changed for the worse. But in his mind, his Chosen Council was to blame. They had taken Anastasia from him, he insisted. Someone had to pay.

CHAPTER 11

The Pretend Abdication

Ivan threatens to quit unless he gets his way—AND IT WORKS.

IVAN'S GROWING TYRANNY angered Russia's noble families. Some fled Russia in fear for their lives. Others appealed to church leaders to speak with the tsar.

Metropolitan Makary had died in 1563 and been replaced by a man named Afanasy. The tsar had chosen the new metropolitan because of his loyalty. But Afanasy was not afraid to criticize Ivan. "No

Christian tsar has the right to treat human beings like animals," he said.

By 1564, Ivan seemed to have lost the support of the ruling classes all across Russia. But the tsar had a plan to force his critics into silence. He set it in motion on December 3, 1564.

On that Sunday, the people of Moscow saw hundreds of sleds pull up to the Kremlin. Servants walked out of the palace with loads of royal treasures. They carried icons, books, gold, jewels, clothes, and furniture. Everything was packed into the sleds under armed guard. Then the tsar and his family drove off into the bitter cold. So did dozens of followers and their families.

The crowd watched in amazement. Where was the tsar going?

On December 21, the tsar's party reached its final stop, about 60 miles northeast of Moscow. They settled into a hunting lodge called Alexandrova Sloboda.

The reason for Ivan's strange behavior became clear a couple of weeks later. On January 3, a messenger

IVAN HAD AMASSED MORE POWER than any ruler in Russia's
history. But could he sway public opinion against the boyars?

arrived in Moscow with two letters. The first letter was addressed to the nobles and church officials. In it, Ivan accused them of every crime possible. They had committed treason, stolen money from the government, and protected traitors, he claimed. The letter went on to say that the tsar was tired of the plots against him. He was giving up his throne "with a heavy heart." He would travel "wherever God may lead him."

Ivan's second letter was addressed to Russia's common people. Large, tense crowds gathered in Kremlin Square to hear it read aloud. In it, Ivan said he had no problem with them. But the boyars and church officials were ruining Russia. He reminded people of the terrible years of boyar rule. He hinted that life in Russia would get much worse without him.

In the coming days, the people of Moscow grew restless. They believed that the boyars had driven the tsar away.

A rumor spread that the people were preparing an attack on the boyars. Russia's ruling families backed down in fear. Metropolitan Afanasy and the boyars quickly sent envoys to Alexandrova Sloboda. They begged Ivan to return to Moscow. The tsar was told he could "govern as he pleased, and . . . punish traitors at his discretion."

Ivan had gambled and won. He had ignored the boyars and appealed directly to the people. He now had the power to do whatever he liked.

The 34-year-old tsar returned to Moscow in mid-February. Crowds lined the streets leading up to the Kremlin. People wept and prayed in thanks. They fell to their knees in the deep snow.

But Ivan hardly looked victorious. He had lost weight. His shoulders were hunched. Much of his hair and beard had fallen out or been pulled out. His face looked gray and wrinkled.

People cheered and church bells rang. Ivan's glassy eyes seemed to notice nothing. They had a crazed look about them.

THE SEVEN WIVES OF IVAN IV

IVAN MARRIED SEVEN WOMEN before he died in 1584. The Orthodox Church did not allow people to have more than three marriages. But Ivan bullied the church into accepting his wives.

Anastasia Romanovna
Years married: 1547–1560
Fate: Died of disease
Children: Six children; only Ivan and Feodor lived beyond infancy.

Maria Temriukovna
Years married: 1561–1569
Fate: Died of disease or poisoning
Children: One son who did not survive

Marfa Sobakina
Years married: 1571
Fate: Died of illness after 16 days of marriage

Anna Koltovskaya
Years married: 1572–1575
Fate: Banished to a convent for failing to produce children

Anna Vassilchikova
Years married: 1575–1577
Fate: Died of illness

Vasilissa Melentieva
Years married: 1577
Fate: Banished to a convent for alleged adultery

Maria Nagaya
Years married: 1580–1584
Fate: Outlived Ivan
Children: One boy who lived to age nine

IVAN ADMIRES THE BEAUTY of his sixth wife, Vasilissa Melentieva.

CHAPTER 12

The Land Apart

IVAN SPLITS HIS COUNTRY IN HALF and spreads fear across the land.

THE TSAR'S RETURN came at a high price for Russia. Ivan demanded that the country be split in two. He would directly rule a territory called the *oprichnina*, or "land apart." The rest of the country, the *zemshchina*, would be ruled by the boyars. Ivan would oversee all of their actions.

Ivan also created a special crew of bodyguards and policemen. They were called the *oprichniki*, or "men apart."

Few things were more terrifying than the arrival of the *oprichniki*. Each of the tsar's chosen men wore black robes and rode a black horse. Hanging from each man's saddle were a severed dog's head and a broom. The dog's head stood for the constant watchfulness of the *oprichniki*. The broom indicated that their job was to sweep up the tsar's enemies.

The *oprichniki* swore absolute loyalty to Ivan. The tsar came before friends, family, and even country. *Oprichniki* came from all walks of life. Many of their leading members were nobles. Others were commoners. Most were chosen personally by Ivan. They could arrest, steal, torture, and kill as they pleased.

Ivan ordered the *oprichniki* to steal land for his personal use. Without warning, the *oprichniki* would arrive at a house. The family and servants would huddle together in terror. The lucky ones were given new lands, hundreds of miles to the east. Some were allowed to take clothes and possessions. Still others were simply ordered to

ALEXANDROVA SLOBODA SERVED AS CAPITAL of the *oprichnina*, Ivan's personal kingdom. From here, Ivan lived like a monk and oversaw his soldiers' destruction of the boyars.

leave. During the brutal winter of 1565, Ivan turned 12,000 landowners and their families into homeless wanderers.

Oprichniki targeted homes of the wealthy. They received one-quarter of the property of anyone they arrested. This solved two problems for Ivan. It stripped wealth and power from the nobles. And it created a class of men who owed everything to the tsar. Over time, the *oprichniki* took over the richest lands in Russia.

Ivan created a home base for his personal army at Alexandrova Sloboda. This small village became an armed camp, the capital of the *oprichnina*.

Life in Alexandrova was bizarre. It was patterned after the simple life of a monk. Everyone, including Ivan, wore black robes. The *oprichniki* addressed each other as "brother." Everyone rose before dawn for a three-hour church service. Each man carried only practical objects—a lantern, a bowl, and a spoon. Severe beatings awaited anyone who forgot them.

Ivan sang, read, and prayed during the morning service. At 7:00 A.M., all the men got an hour's rest and then started a two-hour service. At 10:00 A.M., the *oprichniki* ate breakfast. Ivan watched and often spoke to the men about the lives of saints. Once his men were done, the tsar ate alone.

But prayer was not the tsar's only pastime. From his new capital, Ivan attacked both his enemies and his friends. He sent the *oprichniki* to bring his victims to Alexandrova. Few people came willingly. A German translator who worked for Ivan watched many of them arrive. He wrote, "A man invited by the tyrant to come to Alexandrova sets out feeling that the Day of Judgment has arrived because no one returns from there."

In the dungeons at Alexandrova Sloboda, the guards often used torture. Ivan liked to be there when it happened. The German translator claimed that the tsar cheered at the sight of blood.

In fact, Ivan was known to turn torture into a kind of sport. He supposedly sewed a nobleman into a bearskin. Then he set hunting dogs after the man. On another occasion, Ivan put seven men armed with spears in an arena. Then he turned seven bears loose in the arena. The men did not last long.

During quieter moments, Ivan tended to the business of governing Russia. He met with ambassadors from other countries. Many of them found the tsar to be educated and charming.

IVAN WATCHES AS A MAN IS FED TO A BEAR. Russians who were ordered to Alexandrova rarely returned.

Evenings at Alexandrova were taken up by dinner and more church services. When bedtime came, Ivan was often restless. Three blind storytellers stayed in his room while he lay in bed. The storytellers told fables and Russian folk tales. They told long stories about ancient kings and heroic deeds. Even with the soothing voices, the tsar reportedly had a hard time sleeping.

The Savior of Pskov

A POOR HOLY MAN
stops Ivan when no one else can.

IVAN WAS CONVINCED he was surrounded by
enemies. In September 1569 his second wife, Maria
died. Ivan felt sure she had been poisoned. The tsar
was also alarmed by news from Sweden. King Erik
XIV had been overthrown and imprisoned. The idea
that people would topple their king horrified Ivan.
He wrote to Queen Elizabeth I of England. He asked
her to give him shelter should his people revolt.

The tsar went to great lengths to protect
himself. He surrounded himself with bodyguards.

He also carried a long wooden staff with a sharp metal point. He used it to stab anyone who displeased him.

The slightest threat could lead to bloodshed. On a cold winter day in 1569, Ivan and some of his men were about to leave the palace. Suddenly, a horse broke its halter and got away from its owner. The owner chased the horse across the road in front of the tsar. Ivan thought the event signaled bad luck. He had the attendant and the horse cut to pieces and thrown in a swamp.

Ivan and his *oprichniki* kept the entire country in a state of fear. "No one knew what his own guilt . . . was supposed to be," one witness recalled. "Everybody went about their affairs as if nothing was the matter. Suddenly a band of killers would descend."

To make things worse, criminals sometimes disguised themselves as *oprichniki*. They robbed and killed as they pleased. Their victims didn't dare protest—in case the thugs were the real thing.

In this atmosphere, best friends and family members turned on one another. Ivan had spies all across the country. "[The tsar] delights in listening to informers," wrote the German translator. "He does not care whether their information is true or false if it provides him with an opportunity to destroy people."

Ivan's paranoia began to send Russia into a downward spiral. On the thinnest evidence, the tsar destroyed the country's most talented leaders. His victims included some of his best military commanders. Without decent leadership, the Russian army suffered serious losses in the Livonian War.

In 1570, these losses pushed Ivan toward his most infamous attack. The tsar needed someone to blame for the failures in Livonia. In 1570, he settled on the leaders of Novgorod, accused them of treason, and destroyed their city.

While Novgorod was still smoldering, Ivan turned on the nearby city of Pskov. His army arrived outside the city walls in early February 1570. News of

IVAN THE TERRIBLE RIDES INTO THE CITY of Pskov.
Ivan's personal soldiers, the *oprichniki*, looted the city before a
holy man convinced Ivan to call them off.

the Novgorod massacres had already reached the people there. That night, the churches in the city became unusually crowded. People wept and prayed for mercy. They embraced each other and said their goodbyes. Few people in Pskov slept that night. They expected to die.

The next day, Ivan entered the city. *Oprichniki* were already looting homes and churches. Then, something unexpected happened. Ivan had an encounter with a "holy fool" named Mikula. Russia was full of these strange mystics. Holy fools often spent their lives traveling, living in extreme poverty. They were said to have a special connection with God.

Outside Mikula's house, Ivan heard a voice booming through the window. "Ivan! Ivan! How much longer will you shed innocent blood? Enough. Go home! Or great misfortune will befall you!"

The tsar went inside to confront Mikula. The holy fool offered Ivan a piece of meat. "I am a Christian," Ivan said. "I do not eat meat during Lent."

"You do much worse!" Mikula answered. "You feed upon human flesh and blood, forgetting not only Lent but God himself!"

As Mikula spoke, the sky outside supposedly began to darken. Thunder boomed in the background. Ivan was convinced it was a sign from God. He ordered his troops to withdraw. Pskov was saved.

C H A P T E R   1 4

End of the Oprichnina

Tartar invasions REVEAL IVAN'S TRUE WEAKNESSES.

IN 1571, IVAN'S RUSSIA WAS IN TERRIBLE SHAPE. The *oprichniki* had been terrorizing the people for seven years. Their raids and land seizures had reduced trade. Farmland lay unused all across the country. Poverty and starvation—always a problem—had grown intolerable. With them came epidemics like bubonic plague and cholera.

Just when it seemed things could not get worse, a

Tartar army from Crimea invaded Russia. Russians once knew how to fight the Tartars. But Ivan's executions had left the army and the government without its best leaders.

The Tartar army, 40,000 strong, advanced swiftly. And this time they had help. Ivan had plenty of enemies among his own people. His enemies joined the Tartars as guides, hoping that a victory would get rid of the tsar and his *oprichniki*.

The tsar quickly gathered an army of 50,000. But his troops were divided between *zemshchina* forces and *oprichnina* forces. The Tartars broke through a hole in the disorganized Russian line. They closed in on Alexandrova and Moscow.

The tsar prepared to flee. He packed up his treasures and his most trusted bodyguards. He headed north to the White Sea. If all was lost, he could catch a ship to England.

Back in Alexandrova, many of the soldiers simply gave up. They retreated in chaos to Moscow. Mobs of armed men jammed the roads leading into the Russian capital. With them were tens of thousands of terrified refugees.

On May 24, the Tartars arrived at the gates of Moscow. The disorganized Russians tried their best to hold off the invaders.

Then, the Crimean khan, Devlet, set fire to the city. As in 1547, strong, dry winds carried the flames. Since Tartar soldiers surrounded the city, there was no place for people to flee. Many tried to hide in cellars or stone buildings. Most of them suffocated in the thick smoke.

Church bells rang throughout Moscow when the attack began. But the fire's roar soon drowned them out. "There was nothing but whirlwinds and such noise as though the heavens should have fallen," one witness remembered. The fire burned Moscow to the ground in about six hours.

Satisfied for now, the Tartars rode back to the Crimea. They carried with them thousands of captives.

The following year, the Tartars attacked again. This time, Ivan had learned a lesson. He combined the *zemshchina* and *oprichnina* forces under a single command. The unified Russian army managed to beat back the Tartars.

Finally, Ivan realized that his seven-year experiment had to end. The *oprichniki* had weakened Russia. It had turned the people against their tsar. It had split the country in half and killed many of its best people.

In the fall of 1572, Ivan banned the *oprichnina*. He had some *oprichniki* leaders killed or imprisoned. He even outlawed all discussion of his failed experiment. People caught using the word *oprichnina* could be arrested and whipped for their crime.

THE SECOND ABDICATION

IN 1575, IVAN GAVE UP THE THRONE AGAIN. This time he actually named a replacement. The new "tsar" was a Christian Tartar named Simeon Bekbulatovich.

No one was fooled. Bekbulatovich might receive ambassadors. People might bow to him. But he never received the tsar's crown. Ivan clearly made the decisions from behind the scenes.

Why did Ivan risk placing someone else on the throne? Nobody knows. We do know that a fortuneteller had predicted that the tsar would die in 1575. Perhaps Ivan was hoping that the stand-in leader would die in his place.

For a time, Ivan got a kick out of calling himself just plain "Ivan Vasilyevich," or "Little Ivan of Moscow." But after almost exactly one year, Ivan became tsar again. Bekbulatovich was given a high-ranking job far from Moscow and faded from history.

PART 4

Decline and Fall

Disaster Strikes

CHASING A DREAM OF EMPIRE leads to humiliating defeats.

YEARS OF MISRULE CAUGHT UP with Ivan in his final years. Failure seemed to pile on top of failure.

Perhaps the biggest disaster was the Livonian War. In the 1570s, Ivan's foreign enemies began to unite. Sweden joined forces with Poland and Lithuania. Their inspirational leader was Stephen Bathory, the king of Poland and Lithuania.

Bathory was crowned in 1576. From the start, Ivan hated him. Bathory had been elected by Polish nobles. The idea of such an election disgusted Ivan. In his view, true kings did not need to be chosen by their people. They received their authority from God.

Ivan was furious when this elected king began winning the Livonian War. With the full

STEPHEN BATHORY, the elected king of Poland-Lithuania, resisted Ivan's invasion of Livonia.

KING BATHORY BESIEGES PSKOV. Although the king failed to take the city, he won many other battles against Ivan.

support of his people, Bathory organized an army. Then he hammered away at the Russian-held cities in Livonia.

During this time, Bathory and Ivan communicated often by messenger. The Polish king enjoyed insulting the Russian leader. He refused to refer to Ivan as "tsar." All Bathory's letters were addressed to the "grand prince."

In his letters, Bathory taunted Ivan. At one point, the tsar complained about the way the Poles treated the bodies of Russian soldiers. "You accuse me of abusing the dead," Bathory replied. "I do not abuse them. You, however, torture the living. Which is worse?"

The Polish king even challenged Ivan to a personal battle. "Choose a time and place and meet me on horseback and we shall fight one another!" he declared. "God will crown the better one with victory!"

At one time, Ivan might have speared the messenger who brought him such a letter. Now he could only slump on his throne. "Send greetings to your sovereign from us," he told the messenger.

Ivan had started the Livonian War to enrich Russia. Instead, it bankrupted the country. Desperate for money, the tsar demanded payments from landowners. The landowners, in turn, demanded more from the peasants who worked their farms. Some of these peasants fled. Many others died of starvation or disease. "No one lives in [the villages]," an Italian visitor noted. "The fields are deserted and the forest growth over them is fresh."

The flight from the land alarmed Ivan and his nobles. In 1581, the tsar restricted the peasants' right to leave their farms. This law overturned an old tradition. Peasants had always been allowed to find new landlords after the harvest each November. After Ivan's death, this law became permanent. Russia's peasants had become serfs—slaves to the land. Serfdom would continue in Russia until 1861.

ACCIDENTAL CONQUEST

IVAN HAD WANTED HIS EMPIRE TO GROW WESTWARD, toward Europe. Instead, it grew eastward into Siberia.

Throughout the 1500s, a Tartar tribe controlled the vast territory of Siberia. A wealthy Russian family named the Stroganovs ruled the land around the border. In 1581, the Stroganovs organized an army of thieves and outlaws. They pushed across the Ural Mountains and stormed into Siberia.

ERMAK TIMOFEEVICH, leader of the bandit army in Siberia

When Ivan heard about the raid, he was furious. He threatened to have the Stroganovs executed if they refused to end the war.

But in 1583, the leader of the bandit army arrived in Moscow. He showed Ivan a load of beautiful furs. And he humbly offered all the land he had conquered to the tsar.

Ivan instantly pardoned the Stroganovs and their army. He accepted their gifts. Russia had just begun its conquest of one of the richest regions of the world.

CHAPTER 16

A Death in the Family

Ivan's rage STRIKES TOO CLOSE TO HOME.

TSAR IVAN IV INSPIRED FEAR in everyone, including his oldest son, Tsarevich Ivan. In 1581, the heir to the throne was 27 years old. The tsar kept a close watch over his son. Every friend the young prince made seemed to his father like a possible traitor. The tsar killed or imprisoned many of them. He even forced his son to give up his first and second wives. And several family members of the prince's third wife, Elena, were executed.

Tsar Ivan had mixed feelings about his older son. The young man was smart and charming. He had been trained in the affairs of government. He was also Ivan's best hope to continue the family's rule over Russia. Ivan's younger son, Feodor, was kind but childlike. He may have been mentally disabled.

On the other hand, young Ivan dared to disagree with his father publicly. He pushed hard to continue the war in Livonia. He even volunteered to lead troops there. The offer was probably an attempt to shame his father. The tsar had a reputation for running from battles.

Young Ivan was also more popular than his father. The constant tyranny of the past two decades had exhausted the Russian people. Many looked forward to the day when a new tsar would take over. Their affection for the prince made Ivan jealous. He saw his son as one more threat to his power.

On November 14, 1581 Ivan's resentment led to murder. The tsar found Elena and his son sitting in a room in the Kremlin Palace. Elena was several months pregnant with the tsar's grandchild.

Apparently, Ivan felt that his daughter-in-law was not dressed properly. He flew into a rage and began hitting and kicking her. Young Ivan moved to stop his father. Furious, Ivan picked up his metal-tipped staff. He hit his son in the side of the head.

Young Ivan slumped to the floor. Blood poured from his wound onto the rich carpet. Doctors rushed in and tried to save the heir to the throne. But his skull was cracked. He died five days later. Elena miscarried and died not long after. In just a few moments, Ivan had wiped out his own dynasty.

The tsar's grief was awesome. "[He] tore his hair and beard like a mad man, lamenting and mourning," a witness wrote. He wailed and cried. He scratched the walls with his fingernails. Unable to sleep, he spoke with his son at night as if he were there.

After his son's burial, Ivan began keeping a series of lists. The lists included the names of all the people he

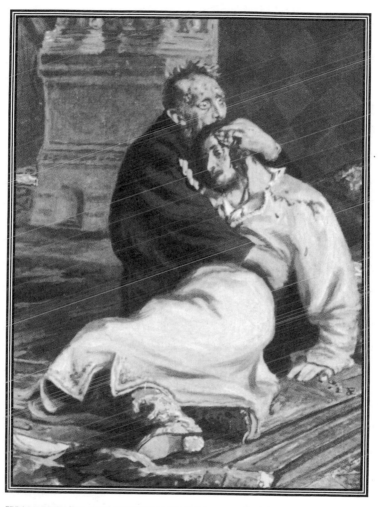

IVAN HOLDS HIS DYING SON. The tsar had been jealous of his
son, yet young Ivan's death overwhelmed the tsar with grief.

had killed——at least the ones he remembered. Many of the names were followed by "with his wife" or "with his sons." At least 3,000 people were on the lists. Many were listed simply as "names known only to God."

Ivan pardoned each of the people on the lists. Then he sent copies of the lists to monasteries all across Russia. He included gifts of money to the monks. He asked clergymen to pray over each of the names.

Was Ivan finally feeling the weight of his crimes? Was he looking for forgiveness? Was he trying to save his own soul?

Possibly. Despite his crimes, Ivan always considered himself a devout Christian. Yet he was also a politician. He knew he had made plenty of enemies during his reign. Many of Russia's most powerful families had lost sons and daughters to Ivan's rage. These people could make life difficult for Feodor when he took over as tsar. Perhaps Ivan hoped his lists——a kind of apology——would help his son maintain the family's hold on Russia after Ivan was gone.

C H A P T E R   1 7

Final Prayers

ILLNESS FINALLY CONQUERS
Ivan the Terrible.

IN EARLY 1584, A COMET APPEARED in the sky above Moscow. Servants bundled their aging tsar in furs and carried him outside. In the cold night air the tsar saw the comet through the domes of two cathedrals. Its tail formed a faint cross. "This," he muttered, "is a sign of my death."

The tsar's death was on everyone's mind. His health had been declining for years. Ivan suffered from a disease that caused great pain in his joints and spine. He could barely walk. Servants carried him everywhere in a chair. A bowel ailment caused his body to swell and stink. The tsar seemed to be rotting from the inside out.

Ivan still found some joy in his life. He liked to be carried to his treasure room. There, he spent hours with the gold, gems, and other valuables he had collected. He liked to think about the magical powers the various gems were supposed to have. Diamonds were said to control anger. Rubies helped heal "corrupt blood." Sapphires increased courage. Turquoise and coral detected poison.

As the winter of 1584 wore on, Ivan's health faded. Sometimes he called out for his son, Ivan, as though the prince were alive.

Doctors could do nothing. Ivan sent word to all the monasteries in Russia. He asked the monks to pray to "forgive his wickedness" and "grant him a cure."

Ivan also consulted fortunetellers. Aides asked 60 of them to provide daily updates on the tsar's fate. Supposedly these men agreed that Ivan would die on

March 18. The fortunetellers were threatened with death if they were wrong.

On March 18, Ivan went through his normal routine. Ointments and rubs were followed by

THE TSAR SEEMED TO BE ROTTING from the inside out. And at night, he was haunted by memories of the people he had killed.

A FORTUNETELLER (right) foretells Ivan's death (seated). The tsar was obsessed with his death. He consulted fortunetellers, tried magical remedies, and begged God to forgive him.

steaming baths. He spent at least four hours in the bath. "According to the fortunetellers," he told an aide, "today is the day I should draw my last breath. But I feel my strength reviving. So let the imposters prepare for death themselves!"

Ivan's aide went to the fortunetellers. He pointed out that Ivan seemed as strong as ever. The day was not yet over, they said.

Ivan sat down to play chess. The first sign of trouble came as he set up the pieces. The king and queen fell over. Seconds later, Ivan made a loud cry and collapsed. There was yelling and alarm. Servants and doctors came rushing into the room. They moved the tsar to his bed. But nothing could be done.

Ivan the Terrible was dead.

Wicked?

Ivan's 50-year reign was over. Power in Russia now lay with Feodor, Ivan's son. As expected, he became a pawn of his advisers. Most people accepted this readily. Feodor's easy laughter and kind manner made for a pleasant change.

After Feodor's death, the Romanov family came to power. They would rule Russia for 300 years.

Many of the Romanov tsars truly admired Ivan. After all, he had founded the Russian empire by conquering the Tartars. He also redefined what it meant to be the ruler of Russia. Before Ivan, the grand prince of Moscow had only a weak hold over the country's noble families. Ivan declared himself tsar and extended his power over millions of people.

Ivan's reputation lasted even after the Romanov dynasty fell in 1917. That year Russia became the Soviet Union, a communist country.

Three decades later, moviemaker Sergei Eisenstein

tried to capture Ivan's reign on film. But Soviet leader Joseph Stalin—himself a ruthless dictator—thought the movie was too critical. Stalin considered Ivan his "teacher," and he wanted Eisenstein to change his movie. "Ivan the Terrible was cruel," Stalin told the filmmaker. "You can show he was cruel. But you must show why he needed to be cruel."

Did Ivan "need" to be cruel? Most tyrants justify their crimes by insisting that they are saving their people from a worse fate. Ivan did the same. He constantly reminded people how terrible things were during his childhood. Russia needed a strong ruler, he insisted. Otherwise it would return to the chaos of boyar rule.

But under Ivan, violence only led to more violence. He executed people because he believed he had enemies everywhere. The more people he killed, the more enemies he made. The more enemies he made, the more his paranoia seemed justified.

In the end, it may come down to a simple question: Does anything justify the killing of innocent people?

Timeline of Terror

1530

December 1533: Vasily III, Ivan's father, dies.

December 28, 1543: Ivan begins to assert his power, orders the arrest and death of Prince Andrei Shuisky.

February 3, 1547: Ivan marries Anastasia Romanovna.

1550: Reforms begin to take power from the church and the nobles and give it to the tsar.

March 1553: Ivan falls ill. Many of his advisers refuse to swear allegiance to his infant son, Dmitri.

January 1558: Livonian War begins.

Late 1560: Ivan accuses Adashev and Sylvester of treason and removes them from his council.

January 1565: The *oprichnina* and *zemshchina* are established.

January 1570: Ivan's troops massacre the residents of Novgorod.

August 1579: King Stephen Bathory begins successful campaigns against Russians in Livonia.

April 3, 1538: Ivan's mother Elena dies. The Shuisky and Belsky families battle for power.

January 16, 1547: Ivan is crowned tsar.

June 21, 1547: Fire destroys much of Moscow.

October 1552: Ivan's armies capture Kazan.

June 1553: Dmitri dies.

August 7, 1560: Tsarina Anastasia dies.

December 1564: Ivan threatens to step down.

1568: Worst period of mass killings during Ivan's reign.

Fall 1572: Ivan bans the *oprichniki* after victory over Crimean Tartars.

November 19, 1581: Ivan kills his oldest son and heir, Tsarevich Ivan.

1584

Glossary

boyars (BOI-urz) *noun* wealthy landowners who were the highest-ranking nobles during the time of Ivan IV

bubonic plague (byoo-BON-ik PLAYG) *noun* a deadly infectious disease spread by fleas infected by rats

chaos (KAY-oss) *noun* total confusion

cholera (KOL-ur-uh) *noun* a dangerous disease that causes severe sickness and diarrhea

conquest (KON-kwest) *noun* the act of conquering

convict (kuhn-VIKT) *verb* to find or prove that someone is guilty of a crime

coronation (cor-uh-NAY-shun) *noun* the ceremony in which a royal leader is crowned

corrupt (kuh-RUHPT) *adjective* dishonest in business or government dealings

democracy (di-MOK-ruh-see) *noun* a system of government in which the people choose their leaders through elections

devout (di-VOUT) *adjective* deeply religious

empire (EM-pire) *noun* a group of countries that have the same ruler

execute (ek-suh-KYOOT) *verb* to kill someone as punishment for a crime

exploit (ek-SPLOIT) *verb* to make use of unfairly for one's own advantage

heir (AIR) *noun* the person next in line to the throne

icon (EYE-kon) *noun* a picture of a holy figure

khan (KON) *noun* a ruler of Turkish or Tartar tribes during the time of Ivan IV

khanate (KON-ate) *noun* a region ruled by a khan

leper (LEP-uhr) *noun* a person who has leprosy, an infectious disease caused by bacteria that attack the skin, nerves, and muscles

massacre (MASS-uh-kur) *noun* the brutal killing of a very large number of people

metropolitan (met-ruh-POL-uh-tuhn) *noun* the head of the Russian Orthodox Church

noble (NOH-buhl) *noun* a person born into a wealthy family with the highest social rank in a society

oprichniki (oh-preech-NEEK-ee) *noun* members of the special police force Ivan assembled to terrorize the people of Russia

oprichnina (oh-preech-NEE-na) *noun* a separate state within Russia that Ivan created to be completely under his personal control; it included a small section of Moscow, a part of the Kremlin, about 20 selected towns, and some scattered stretches of farmland and forest

paranoia (pa-ruh-NOI-uh) *noun* irrational suspiciousness

revolution (rev-uh-LOO-shuhn) *noun* an uprising by the people of a country that changes the country's system of government

serf (SURF) *noun* in Russia, a peasant laborer who was tied to the land and was forced to work for a noble landowner

sovereign (SOV-ruhn) *noun* the supreme leader of a country

streltsy (STREL-tzee) *noun* the units of rifle-carrying armed guardsmen formed by Ivan; *streltsy* is the Russian word for "shooter"

treason (TREE-zuhn) *noun* the crime of betraying one's country by spying for another country or helping an enemy during a war

tsar (ZAR) *noun* the emperor of Russia

tsarevich (ZAR-eh-vitch) *noun* the heir to the throne in Russia

tsarina (zar-EE-nuh) *noun* the wife of a tsar

vengeance (VEN-juhnss) *noun* punishment inflicted in retaliation for an injury or offense

zemshchina (zem-SHEE-nuh) *noun* the parts of Russia outside the *oprichnina* that Ivan set aside for the boyars to rule

FIND OUT MORE

Here are some books and Web sites with more information about Ivan IV and his times.

BOOKS

Butson, Thomas G. Ivan the Terrible (World Leaders Past and Present). New York: Chelsea House, 1987. (112 pages)
A fascinating exploration of Ivan's difficult childhood, his role as a reformer, and his reign of terror.

Nardo, Don. Ivan the Terrible (History's Villains). Farmington Hills, MI: Blackbirch Press, 2006. (112 pages)
A detailed account of the life of Ivan IV.

Rogers, Stillman D. Russia (Enchantment of the World, Second Series). New York: Children's Press, 2002. (144 pages)
Describes the history, geography, and people of Russia

Strickler, James E. Russia of the Tsars. San Diego: Lucent Books, 1998. (96 pages)
This book covers the history of Russia under the tsars, from the 1500s to 1917.

WEB SITES

http://encarta.msn.com/encyclopedia_761561311/Ivan_IV_Vasilyevich.html
MSN Encarta's online encyclopedia article about Ivan IV is written by University of Chicago professor Richard Hellie, a noted Russian history scholar.

http://russia.nypl.org/level1.html
This New York Public Library Web site, Russia Engages the World, *places Ivan's reign in context.*

http://www.pbs.org/weta/faceofrussia/intro.html
This companion Web site to the PBS series The Face of Russia *offers an excellent timeline and other resources.*

For Grolier subscribers:
http://go.grolier.com/ searches: Ivan IV; Kazan; Astrakhan, Crimea; Stephen Bathory; oprichnina; Kremlin; Russia

INDEX

Adashev, Aleksei, 45, 47, 58, 62, 74–76

Afanasy Metropolitan (head of Orthodox Church), 78, 82

Agrafena (nanny of Ivan IV), 20

Alexandrova Sloboda, 79, 82, 86–90, 98

Anastasia, Tsarina (first wife of Ivan IV), 39, 41, 56, 59, 64, 65, 67, 69, 71, 75-77

Arctic Circle, 76

Astrakhan, 61

Baltic Sea, 62

Bathory, Stephen, 104–107

Bekbulatovich, Simeon, 101

Belsky family, 19, 24, 25, 29

boyars (noblemen), 18–21, 22, 23, 25–27, 43, 66, 80–82, 84

bubonic plague, 97

Caspian Sea, 61

Chancellor, Richard, 60–62

cholera, 97

Chosen Council, 44, 45, 47, 57–58, 68

Christianity, 52, 67, 79, 95

council of advisers, 18, 20–21, 25

Crimea, 55, 98, 99

Denmark, 63

Dmitri (son of Ivan IV and Anastasia), 56, 57-59, 69

Elena, Grand Princess of Moscow (mother of Ivan IV), 17–20, 66

Elizabeth I, 62, 91

England, 60–62, 91, 98

Erik XIV, 91

Estonia, 62

Feodor (son of Ivan IV and Anastasia), 64, 111, 120

fortunetellers, 116–118

Glinskaya, Elena (mother of Ivan IV), 17–20, 66

Glinsky family, 31, 43, 44

Glinsky, Mikhail, 18

Glinsky, Yuri, 43

Guirey, Devlet, 99

icons, religious, 31, 33, 64, 79

Ivan III (grandfather of Ivan IV), 16, 22, 59

Ivan IV, Tsar
  abdications of, 69, 78, 101
  army of, 12, 50–54, 61, 68, 93, 98
  as grand prince of Moscow, 22, 66
  as tsar, 37, 44, 46–48, 55, 67
  assessment of, 120–122
  childhood of, 13, 16, 17, 18–21, 23–26, 66
  coronation of, 36–38, 67
  criticism of, 44, 78–79
  cruelty of, 11–13, 40–41, 44, 57, 67–70, 76–78, 85–89, 92–96, 110–112
  death of, 71, 119
  education of, 31–32
  empire, expansion of, 38, 47–48, 61, 109
  enemies of, 11, 48, 57, 74, 91, 98, 104
  health of, 57–58, 82, 115–119
  nobles, teenage gang of, 30–31, 67
  reforms by, 48
  religious practices of, 31–33, 67, 68, 86–87, 90, 95, 114, 116
  unstable behavior of, 32, 56–57, 69–71, 74–77, 79, 82, 86, 91–93, 110–114
  victories of, 54–57, 59, 61, 68, 69, 82, 93
  wives of, 39, 67, 77, 83, 91

Ivan, Tsarevich (son of Ivan IV and Anastasia), 59, 71, 110-111, 112-114

Josef, Metropolitan, 23–24

Kazan, 49–54, 68

khanates (kingdoms), 48

Koltovskaya, Anna (fourth wife of Ivan IV), 83

Kremlin, 25, 28, 41, 58, 66, 79, 82

Kremlin Square, 30, 31, 43, 46, 80

Latvia, 62

Lithuania, 104

Livonia, 62–64, 104–107, 111

London, 30, 68

Makary, Metropolitan (head of the Orthodox Church), 38, 78

Makhmet, Khan Yediger, 53, 54

Maria (daughter of Ivan IV and Anastasia), 56

Maria (second wife of Ivan IV), 77, 83, 91

Melentieva, Vassilissa (sixth wife of Ivan IV), 83

Mikula, "holy fool," 95

Moscow, 16, 22, 24, 28, 30, 31, 42–44, 99

Moscow River, 28, 42

Nagaya, Maria (seventh wife of Ivan IV), 83

Narva, 63

Novgorod, 11–13, 44, 70, 93, 95

omen, 41, 115

oprichniki (men apart), 84–88, 97–98, 100

oprichnina (land apart), 84, 86, 87, 98–100

Orthodox Church. See Russian Orthodox Church

plague, bubonic, 97

poisoning, accusations of, 75, 91

Poland, 11–12, 63, 66, 104–107

Polish king, 104–107

Pskov, 41, 44, 93–96, 106

Repnin, Prince Mikhail, 77

Russia, 11, 13, 24, 26–28, 36–38, 46–48, 61–63, 80–81, 84, 88, 93, 97–100, 106–108, 111, 120

Russian Orthodox Church, 23, 33, 46, 69

serfdom, 108

Sheksna River, 58

Shuisky, Prince Andrei, 26–27, 29

Shuisky, Prince Ivan, 21

Shuisky family, 19, 24–26, 29

Siberia, 109

slavery, 50, 53, 68, 70

Sobakina, Marfa (third wife of Ivan IV), 83

St. Basil's Cathedral, 69

Staritsky, Prince Vladimir,

57–58

streltsy (shooters), 50, 51

Stroganovs, 109

Sweden, 63, 91, 104

Sylvester, Father, 44, 58, 62, 74–76

Tartars, 48–50, 52, 55, 61, 98–101, 109

taxes, 24, 47, 50, 68

Temriukovna, Maria (second wife of Ivan IV), 77, 83, 91

Timofeevich, Ermale, 109

trade, 60–63, 97

Ural Mountains, 109

Vasily III, Grand Prince of Moscow (father of Ivan IV), 16–18, 21, 22

Vassilchikova, Anna (fifth wife of Ivan IV), 83

vegetable lamb, 61

Volga River, 50, 61

Volkhov River, 12

Vorontzov, Feodor, 26

White Sea, 76, 98

witchcraft, accusations of, 19, 31, 43, 75, 76

Yuri (brother of Ivan IV), 17, 20, 21

zemshchina, 84, 98, 100

Author's Note and Bibliography

Ivan the Terrible's Russia can be tough for modern minds to grasp. The frigid climate was similar to Alaska's. Russians were either very rich or very poor, with few people in between. People at the time firmly believed in things that we consider outdated, such as witchcraft. Even the country's name was different. Back then, Russia was widely called Muscovy.

Several books guided me through this strange land. Here is a list of the most helpful:

Benson, Bobrick. **Fearful Majesty: The Life and Reign of Ivan the Terrible.** New York: Putnam's Sons, 1987.

Esper, Thomas, ed. **The Land and Government of Muscovy: A 16th-Century Account.** Stanford, CA: Stanford University Press, 1967.

Pavlov, Andrei and Maureen Perrie. **Ivan the Terrible.** London: Pearson Longman, 2003.

Payne, Robert and Nikita Romanoff. **Ivan the Terrible.** New York: Thomas Y. Crowell Co., 1975.

Schlicting, Albert. "A Brief Account of the Character and Brutal Rule of Ivan Vasil'evich, Tyrant of Muscovy." Edited and translated by Hugh F. Graham, Canadian-American Slavic Studies, Summer 1975.

Troyat, Henri. **Ivan the Terrible.** ed. and translated by Joan Pinkham. London: Phoenix Press, 2001.

Worth, Michael. **Everyday Life Through the Ages.** London: Reader's Digest, 1992.

Special thanks to editor Tod Olson for his patience and direction. Thanks also to my wife, Debra, and son, Zachary, for allowing me to spend so much time trying to understand Ivan.

—Sean Price